EMPLOYER CONTROLS
OVER PRIVATE LIFE

RONALD C. MCCALLUM holds the Blake Dawson Waldron professorship in industrial law at the University of Sydney, and he is special counsel in industrial law at the law firm of Blake Dawson Waldron. His books include *Australian Labour Law: Cases and Materials* (with Marilyn Pittard).

Other Frontlines

A Bill of Rights for Australia
George Williams

Australia's Economic Revolution
John Edwards

Deadlock or Democracy: The Future of the Senate
Brian Costar(ed), with Meg Lees, Helen Coonan, John Faulkner and
Harry Evans

Death of Broadcasting: Media's Digital Future
Jock Given

Gambling Government: The Economic and Social Impacts
Michael Walker

Saving the Environment: What It Will Take
Ted Trainer

Taxing Times: A Guide to Australia's Tax Debate
John Quiggin

The Wik *Debate: Its Impact on Aborigines, Pastoralists and Miners*
Frank Brennan

RONALD McCALLUM

EMPLOYER
CONTROLS OVER
PRIVATE LIFE

UNSW
PRESS

A UNSW Press book

Published by
University of New South Wales Press Ltd
University of New South Wales
Sydney 2052 Australia
www.unswpress.com.au

National Library of Australia
Cataloguing-in-Publication entry:

McCallum, R.C. (Ronald Clive).
Employer controls over private life.

Bibliography.
ISBN 0 86840 450 0.

1. Work and family. 2. Industrial relations. 3. Employees
— Effect of technological innovations on. I. Title.
(Series: Frontlines (Sydney)).

331.04

Printer Southwood Press, Marrickville

| CONTENTS

Acknowledgments 4

1 Working life and home life 5

2 Changing work and technology 9

3 The medieval roots of employment 15
relations

4 Employer controls over the standard 21
employee

5 The rise of professional and staff 29
employment

6 Employer controls over professional 35
and staff employees

7 Restoring the balance 50

List of cases 53

Bibliography 56

ACKNOWLEDGMENTS

This book grew out of a seminar paper which I delivered on Friday, 27 March 1998 at the sixth Annual Labour Law Conference which was jointly held by the Faculty of Law of the University of Sydney and the Australian Centre for Industrial Relations Research and Training also of the University of Sydney. I wish to thank Associate Professor Ron Callis and Paul Ronfeldt for their assistance with my seminar paper and with the conference.

In writing the book, I also wish to thank my assistants, Joel Butler and Melissa Tornatore, for their invaluable help. As a member of the Industrial Relations and Employment Law Group of the national law firm of Blake Dawson Waldron, I owe a great deal to my colleagues for their assistance and encouragement, and I especially wish to acknowledge the help which I received from Lea Constantine, Adrian Morris, Belinda Smith and Petra Stirling.

I dedicate this small volume to my wife, Dr Mary Crock, and to our children — Gerard, Daniel and Kate — because their encouragement and unconditional love has bestowed upon me the gift of a balanced and fulfilled life. Our children are now at primary school and Mary and I are both engaged in full-time professional employment. I am a part-time labour law professor and I also practise labour law on a part-time basis. Mary is an immigration law academic, who is engaged in teaching and in writing, and who is deeply involved in immigration issues. My blindness adds a further dimension to the dynamics of our family life. At times, I find work overwhelming and am often disturbed by our pace of life as Mary and I seek to balance our careers, the needs of our growing children and our own private desires and aspirations. Briefly put, I am battling with the intrusion of our work into the life of our family, and it is because of this experience that I wrote this book. I wish to argue for a restoration of a workable balance between employment and home because this synergy is essential to a fulfilled and democratic Australia.

Ronald C. McCallum

1 | WORKING LIFE AND HOME LIFE

In the last half of the 19th century, when the Australian trade union movement was campaigning for the eight-hour day, its slogan was 'eight hours work, eight hours sleep and eight hours play'. The unions were fighting against excessive working hours which were products of agricultural toil and of 19th century industrial employment. The thinking behind this slogan was that, for men at least, there was much more to life than the undertaking of paid work. The slogan presupposed that there was a type of 'divine' balance between work, rest and leisure. When an employee was at work, her or his activities were controlled by the employer, but an employee's domestic, social, sporting and political activities outside work hours were not the employer's business. In other words, until the last quarter of this century it made sense to divide up the lives of workers into working lives and home lives. For Australia's factory workers and even for the vast bulk of clerical employees, once the 'knock off' whistle blew, working life came to a sharp end and home life commenced. The concept of receiving overtime pay loadings made sense because the employee was selling part of her or his precious home time to the employer.

At the turn of the millennium, however, the concept of the eight-hour day for five days a week appears to belong to a bygone age. In a 1998 study titled *Australia at Work*, the Australian Centre for Industrial Relations Research and Training of the University of Sydney found that only just over one-third of Australian workers are employed for between 35 and 40 hours per week. One-third of full-time workers actually work extended hours, whether on long shifts, for overtime or merely as part of their obligations as professional and staff employees. On the other hand, approximately a quarter of the workforce — 75 per cent of whom are women — are employed on a part-time basis. For other employees — such as those in the cleaning and hospitality industries — changing rosters and broken shifts, where early morning and late afternoon work may be required, make up the normal working week.

Over the last 25 years — and more especially as we approach the year 2000 — it has become clear that for increasing numbers of employees, the sharp divide between working life and home life no longer exists, as we seek to balance our career aspirations and our family responsibilities in changing work conditions.

This book focuses upon professional employment and what I shall call 'staff employment'. Professional employees undertake work in one of the growing list of professional callings, while those engaged in staff employment are not simply employees exchanging time for money, but staff members of employing enterprises, committed to certain duties and obligations. Although my focus is on these two groups of employees, I shall not exclude the obligations which are imposed upon other workers. This is because the increase in employer controls over professional and staff employees will inevitably expand to cover other types of employees.

In professional and staff employment, which are products of our service-oriented economy, my contention is that the balance has tipped too far in favour of working life and has left insufficient room for home life. There are two aspects to this intrusion. First, many professional and staff employees are employed to perform tasks rather than for set working hours so that work now intrudes into evenings and weekends. Second, notions of professionalism are curtailing the freedom of action of more and more employees even outside of working hours. More and more corporations and firms have high expectations of employee behaviour, in an endeavour to project to the public at large a responsible corporate image. Many employees have as part of their employment contracts, written policies and/or codes of conduct which to varying degrees limit their rights of free speech.

My aim is to explore the controls which employers are now exerting on employees whether during or outside their hours of work. I believe that for the good of Australian working women and men, there needs to be a restoration of that healthy balance between working life and home life. In a democratic society, working women and men require what I call 'home space' to nurture their relationships and to parent their children; to engage in hobbies, recreational and sporting activities; for spiritual contemplation and reflection; to join clubs, churches, political parties, community bodies and environmental organisations and so on.

Without time for these activities, community life loses that whole-someness which is the birthright of our future generations.

As a professional labour lawyer, my interest is in the legal rules which have brought about this imbalance between work and home. These rules had their origin in feudal England where the master had dominion over his servants, but they changed radically during the Industrial Revolution when large numbers of people were employed in mines, mills and factories. Employment was then governed by contract law (rather than by status) and the rise of the employment contract began. In the 20th century, the contractual rules of employment have been supplemented by statute law and by the rulings of our industrial relations tribunals. Yet, the obligations of employers and employees to each other are still largely governed by the express and implied terms of the employment contract. When employers seek to control the private and out-of-hours activities of their employees, it is these employee obligations in the employment contract which are their legal weapons. It appears that modern notions of corporate loyalty and corporate image are being used by the law to increase employer controls over professional and staff employees.

This is not a textbook on the law: rather it is narrowly focused upon those rules which constrain employees whilst they are still employed. I shall not have time to explore the rules which seek to preclude what employees may or may not do once they have left the service of an employer. When and how former employees may be constrained with respect to confidential information of their former employer, or the circumstances in which they may be prevented for a time for working for a competitor will not be discussed here. Those seeking an elaboration of these rules should consult the interesting work of Andrew Stewart of Flinders University (see the bibliography for details). It is important to note that the legal rules which determine employer controls do not operate in a vacuum because each generation of judges reshapes them in the light of changes in the nature of our economy and society.

Over the last 25 years we have witnessed a shift from employment in our manufacturing industries to the emerging service sector of our economy. Areas such as communications, hospitality and consultancies of all shapes and sizes have especially mushroomed in the 1990s. The fax, computer, email and mobile telephone have altered the way we do business, and have enabled work to move from the office to the home. Economic globalisation and increased competition have also affected working life, as discussed in Chapter 2. In the light of these changes, it is timely to reappraise the employee and employer obligations especially with regard to their intrusion into our private lives.

2 | CHANGING WORK AND TECHNOLOGY

When I was a small boy growing up in suburban Melbourne in the 1950s, working life was radically different from what it is today. In fact, things are so different that sitting here keying in these words into this computer with its synthetic speech system, it is difficult for me to recall exactly what life was like only 40 years ago. In my suburb, a majority of men worked in manufacturing industries, in clerical employment or had public sector jobs in the railways and the post office, and worked a standard 40-hour week. Most married women didn't work and, in our suburb at least, professional women were rarities. The labour market was highly regulated by an Australia-wide grid of awards which spelled out the wage rates and working conditions of most employees. The overwhelming majority of workers were employed according to time-service contracts, whereby they were required to be under the employer's control for the standard working week. What the employee did out of working hours was usually not the concern of the employer.

The technology in most workplaces and in the home was relatively simple and unsophisticated by today's standards. Cars, television sets and telephones were becoming household items of ordinary families, but the microwave cooker, CD player and video recorder were unthought of devices, only imaginable within the realms of science fiction.

In the 1990s, changes in the way work is performed (because of technology) and who undertakes it have been far-reaching with major implications for the ability of employees to control their own working lives.

Work at the turn of the millennium

The most significant change in the labour force in recent times has been the increased participation of women (that is, the percentage of females aged 15 and over who are in the workforce), and more especially of married women. In the 1994 *Family Leave Test Case* which was heard by the Australian Industrial Relations

Commission, interesting evidence was presented on who works in the 1990s. In 1947, women comprised less than 25 per cent of the workforce and the majority of working women were unpartnered. By June 1993, however, 42 per cent of Australian employees were women. In 1978, the female participation rate was 43.7 per cent, but by 1993, 52.3 per cent of women were engaged in paid work. Despite the public sector cuts of the 1990s — which have significantly affected female employment — by April 1998 the female participation rate had risen to 53.9 per cent. Of course, many men over the age of 15 are also not in employment, and over the last decade the male participation rate has fallen (Pocock, 1998). In April 1998, 72.8 per cent of men compared to 53.9 per cent of women undertook employment. Ten years ago, the male participation rate was a little higher at 75.9 per cent.

In 1990, 53 per cent of married women undertook paid employment, and 59 per cent of these women had dependent children. At that time, 62 per cent of married men who were in the workforce also had dependent children. It is fair to conclude that no longer is it true for the majority of families with dependent children that the man is the only bread-winner while the woman does only unpaid work in the home.

Another significant change in the labour market is the increased use of part-time employment. Earlier in this century, in order to safeguard full-time jobs many awards made it difficult to hire part-time employees. Over the last 20 years, however, these restrictions have been set aside and there has been an avalanche in the growth of the part-time workforce. In 1998 the Industrial Relations Commission of New South Wales heard the *Part-Time Work Test Case*, which provided evidence that part-time work is the fastest growing area of employment in Australia. In 1966 only 9.8 per cent of workers were part-time employees. By 1997, however, part-time employees comprised 26 per cent of the labour force with 73 per cent of these being women. In fact, 43 per cent of women work on a part-time basis. It now appears that in the typical family with dependent children, the woman undertakes part-time employment. There has also been a proliferation of casual employment with approximately 23 per cent of Australian employees being employed on a casual basis, with most of these casual employees being women. Casual and part-time employment overlap, as almost two-thirds of part-time employees are employed on a casual basis. In August 1995, for example, men held 5 per cent of part-time jobs on a permanent basis and 17.6 per cent on a casual basis. Women held 32.7 per cent of part-time jobs on a permanent basis and 44.6 per cent on a casual basis.

There are two important points to make about women's employment at the end of the 20th century. First, while it is clear that a majority of women now undertake employment outside the home, men have insufficiently altered their domestic habits, so that women still undertake a majority of the household chores and do more than their fair share of rearing children. This places extra pressures upon women, especially when they are involved in professional or staff employment where increased employee duties are placed upon them. Second, while many women choose part-time employment to balance their careers and families, it would be wrong to conclude that most women with partners and children regard part-time employment as the ideal. Statistical surveys and my observations show that for very many women, part-time work is a 'second best' because appropriate full-time jobs are unavailable and, with government cutbacks, childcare is less available and less affordable.

Another fast growing area of the labour market is that of the self-employed. Approximately 11 per cent of the Australian labour force describe themselves as self-employed and two-thirds of these are men. In law, these people are not employees but are independent contractors. There have been many legal decisions on the circumstances when, according to law, a person will be regarded as either an employee or an independent contractor and these are catalogued in the standard labour law texts. The most important factor is the capacity which the person directing the work has to control the person undertaking the work, however the ownership of equipment and the contractual terms of the parties are also relevant. A useful example is the 1996 case of *Vabu Pty Ltd v Commissioner of Taxation* which was decided by the New South Wales Court of Appeal. The question was whether courier drivers who owned their own vehicles were employees of the courier operator. Despite the allocation of the work by the operator and the high level of supervision which the courier operator had over the drivers, the Court came to the view that the drivers were independent contractors. A slight rearrangement of the conditions of work in cases like this one can turn employees into independent contractors and vice versa. In the coming years as enterprises focus even more strongly upon their core activities, they will contract out many of their ancillary functions to independent contractors and this will lead to an increase in the proportion of Australians who are self-employed.

As I remarked in Chapter 1, no longer is the standard 40-hour week employment the norm. One-third of employees work for more than 40 hours, with many being employed for at least 50 hours a week. At the turn of the millennium, in a typical family, the man works for more than 40 hours per week, and the woman undertakes part-time or full-time employment while still doing more than her fair share of the care of children and the running of the household.

Changes in technology

During the last 20 years, we have all been living through what our grandchildren will probably call the computer revolution. So sudden have these changes been that it is difficult to comprehend their impact. I first saw a fax machine in 1979 and it was slow and inaccurate. If it still exists it should be confined to a museum. Today, fax machines are commonplace in offices, hotels and in homes. The compact disc (CD), which gives us brilliantly clear music and has lead to the creation of the CD-ROM for information storage, only became commercially available in the early 1980s.

Of more importance has been the rise of the computer. In the early 1970s, we saw the development of the large mainframe computer system, but in the late 1970s, Apple Computers made a huge advance with the sale of their famous Apple 2. This was the first mass-produced personal computer and was called the home computer. Probably historians will write that the big breakthrough occurred in January 1984 when Apple launched its famous Macintosh 128 range of computers. Instead of using programs based on lists of letters and numbers such as Dos, it worked with a graphic interface where users could operate a mouse to click on the appropriate icon. This type of technology enabled people to master the computer easily because as long as you could click the mouse and type with two fingers you could enter the computer world. The windows environment of the 1990s has built upon this graphic technology to make computers even more accessible. The personal computer has spawned email and the internet and has completely changed the working lives of a majority of Australians.

This type of technology has taken away that distinction between the office and the home which was so familiar to us. After all, it was only a few years ago that business belonged to the office because the documents were housed there, and it was the place where secretaries used typewriters to type up the work. By contrast, in my home, there is a fax machine, two computers, internet and email access, two telephone lines and two mobile phones enabling us to do much of our legal and academic work at home. Today more and more households have personal computers and internet access at home, and many employees now even carry laptop computers to and from the office.

The pace of modern communications has speeded up the work process because in the area of professional employment immediacy is the key. Clients and customers who are able to communicate their demands instantaneously require and expect immediate responses. Documents are no longer sent through the post — instead they are faxed or emailed, and a prompt response follows.

Computer-driven technology has lead to the automation of many manufacturing processes and this is a major reason for the decline of manufacturing jobs in Australia. The increased use of technology has also been a contributing cause of the many employee redundancies which are all too frequently occurring. Manufacturing workers and middle management employees have been the major casualties of the computer revolution.

Globalisation, competition and stress

In the last 15 years, Australian workplaces have undergone significant changes because of Australia's membership of the global economy and because of the increased domestic and foreign competition being faced by most businesses and services. These changes have impacted upon professional and staff employment.

In 1985 Australia floated its dollar and deregulated many aspects of the financial market. These changes, together with tariff reductions, saw our industries entering into the global economy and in order to survive, all businesses have had to become more competitive. This has resulted in employees working harder than ever before, and this is partly why one-third of the workforce is working more than 40 hours a week. Some employees undertake extra work on an overtime basis, while others — mainly professionals and staff employees — are employed on task-performance contracts where the completion of the task and not the hours worked is the determining factor.

These increased pressures have inevitably lead to a partial deregulation of our labour laws. In 1990, a grid of federal and State awards specified on an industry or occupational basis the wage rates and terms and conditions of employment of 80 per cent of the Australian workforce. This meant that employers could only enter into enforceable collective agreements with trade unions under the auspices of industrial tribunals. In 1999 in all of Australia's labour law jurisdictions however, employers are free to enter into enforceable collective agreements directly with their workers. Under federal law and in three of the States (Queensland, Victoria and Western Australia), employers may enter into individual workplace agreements with their employees which bypass existing awards and agreements. Under the Federal Government's *1996 Workplace Relations Act*, awards are now merely safety nets and have been limited in scope to a list of specified items which are known as allowable award matters. This has meant that for many employees, more of their actual terms and conditions of employment are set out in the express and implied terms of common law employment contracts. It is these contractual rules which give employers control over some of the private and out-of-hours activities of their employees.

In the 1980s and 1990s, there has been a sharp decline in manufacturing and an increase in the service sector of our economy in which customer or client satisfaction is the key to success. In this arena, not only is performance very important, but the public image of corporations and businesses is also significant. In seeking to enhance their images, more and more employers are determining what is acceptable behaviour for their employees, both at work and when they are away from work, resulting in high levels of stress. It is clear that work is now harder, longer and more demanding than it has been during the last 50 years. In most families with dependent children, both adults undertake paid employment and fear of job loss is a constant pressure. The world of work is less happy than it has ever been and this unhappiness is impacting upon our private lives.

3 | THE MEDIEVAL ROOTS OF EMPLOYMENT RELATIONS

When I am sitting at my university desk, either preparing classes or correcting student assignments, I rarely reflect upon the employee and employer obligations which bind me as a matter of law. When we become employees, we enter into contracts of employment with our employers. These contracts are, for most of us, the most important contractual relations in our lives. This is because these legal obligations are central to the undertaking of paid work, which is the performance of physical or mental tasks in exchange for money. Wages allow us to feed and clothe ourselves and our dependants. Of equal importance today is that a steady income ensures our ability to obtain lines of credit which give us access to housing, holidays, motor cars and electronic appliances. As the majority of us spend most of our adult waking hours in the performance of paid work, it is sensible to reflect upon those legal rules which govern the undertaking of work.

Origins of employer controls

In the area of Anglo-Australian contract law, the contract of employment is unique as no other contract places such controls on one of the contracting parties. It establishes a regime of employee service which is unparalleled in other contractual relationships and so is known as a contract of service. How did these obligations of service become part and parcel of the modern employment contract? Its history begins in the mid-18th century, just before the Industrial Revolution.

In 1765 Sir William Blackstone published his lectures on English law, but did not include a discussion of labour law in his chapters on contracts. Rather, he placed labour law in his analysis of personal relations because, for Blackstone, labour law was a personal relationship between master and servant, somewhat akin to the relationships (and inherent controls and obligations) between husband and wife and father and child. Servants were required to obey their masters at all times and to act with good faith and fidelity. For their part, masters could discipline their servants just as the law empowered them to chastise their wives and children. As Sezlnick (1969) put it, 'The old law of master and servant looked to the household as a model and saw in its just governance the foundations of orderly society.' Treating the servant as a type of family member did give the worker some advantages. Once hired for the year, the master was required to maintain the servant and dependants in sickness and in health. Yet, the controls which masters had over their servants — especially in and about the manor house — were very extensive, covering dress, behaviour and propriety. As late as 1845 in *Turner v Mason*, for example, the English Court of Exchequer held that a housemaid could be summarily dismissed because she had disobeyed the master's order to remain in the house and instead had visited her dying mother.

These rules, which were based on the status of the individual, grew out of medieval serfdom, and a series of statutes from the *Statute of Labourers* of 1351 up to the 19th century *Master and Servant Acts* cemented these obligations into English law.

It is true that even at the time Blackstone wrote, these old status-based patterns of employment were breaking down, yet for the 19th century judges who placed these master and servant obligations into the contract of employment, the household with its maids and footmen was the employment model with which they were most familiar. This is partly why the old terminology of master and servant law remained with us right up to the early years of the 20th century.

By the end of the Napoleonic wars in 1815, the old forms of employment were being displaced by employment in the new factories which ushered in the Industrial Revolution. The most appropriate manner of accommodating this new form of mass labour into the legal system was to hold that employment contracts existed between factory owner and worker. In 1865, 100 years after Blackstone wrote, the employment contract governed employment. In order to maintain the old but necessary notions of service, obedience and fidelity, mutual trust and confidence, the judges ensured that these aspects of the employment bargain became implied terms of every contract by force of the common law, and this is still the case today.

I would argue that with the higher duties being placed on professional and staff employees, we are witnessing the re-emergence of part of the old status-based rules of employment. In moulding the contract of employment to fit the status of a person as a professional or a staff employee, the judges are reinstituting a type of pre-industrial service into our modern employment law. While the dress, propriety and grooming of factory workers may not have been of much interest to employers, these matters were within the 18th century master's domain because misconduct in these areas brought shame upon the household. Similarly, in today's businesses where service and corporate image are paramount, the dress, propriety, grooming, and even some speech of the employee are the concern of the employer, where the behaviour can be seen to tarnish the corporate image or be perceived as amounting to corporate disloyalty.

Entering the work relationship

Leaving aside short-term casual arrangements, it cannot be too strongly stressed that a contract of employment establishes an ongoing relationship between employee and employer. It is very different from the standard contract for the sale of a car. When A sells a car to B, once the car and money change hands, neither A nor B expect to see one another again because they do not have an ongoing relationship. But when X agrees to become an employee of Y, then X and Y are commencing a relationship which will continue until the contract is terminated.

In the realm of general contract law, contracts of employment possess unique characteristics. The essence of the employment relationship is the performance of tasks in return for payment, however much more is embedded in this arrangement because the performance of tasks requires employee and employer cooperation and employee obedience to a line of command. The concept of obedience is often masked by work arrangements in modern service-oriented employment. The factory hand obeying the foreman is easy to imagine, but such direct orders are rarely issued in professional employment. For most professional and for many staff employees, it is rare to receive orders on a daily basis concerning the performance of tasks. Instead, the cloak of professionalism encloses the command line whereby employees are expected to carry out their functions to high professional standards and exercise their own discretion. Sustained refusal to adhere to these standards will uncloak the command line, leading to warnings and eventually dismissal. In all contracts of employment, obedience to commands is an essential element of the tasks-for-wages agreement.

Employment contracts place duties on employers and employees. Employees have to obey all lawful and reasonable orders and work with care and diligence. This duty of obedience also covers much employee misconduct. Workers are also required to act with good faith and fidelity, that is to conduct themselves in an appropriate manner and not to divulge details of the employer's business. In their turn, employers are obliged to pay wages and to safeguard their employees from unsafe working conditions.

The contract of employment is governed by the common law, and therefore the legal rules concerning these contracts are found in the decisions of the courts of the United Kingdom and Australia. This means that these rules are modified from time to time when courts hand down decisions dealing with the application and interpretation of these rules. In 1997, for example, in *Malik and Mahmud v Bank of Credit and Commerce International*, the English House of Lords — the highest court in the United Kingdom — held that in all employment contracts employers were required not to do anything which would destroy the trust and confidence which existed between them and their employees. In this case, senior officers of the defendant bank had engaged in widespread corrupt activities. When the plaintiff employees, who knew nothing about the corrupt conduct, were made redundant, they were unable to obtain employment in the banking industry as the extent of the defendant bank's corruption became known. The House of Lords held that the corruption of the bank breached its duty as an employer to maintain an obligation of mutual trust and confidence with its employees.

It is clear from this holding that a similar obligation is placed upon employees who also may not destroy the mutual trust and confidence between them and their employers. In Australia, the courts have been reasoning along similar lines, and in my view the House of Lords decision represents the law in this country.

Restricted freedom

The major feature of labour law throughout this century has been the restrictions on freedom of contract, and the supplementation of employment conditions by statute law and by the pronouncements of industrial relations tribunals. For example, statutes from the 1970s to the 1990s now prohibit employers and employees from discriminating against persons on the grounds of race, gender, sexual preference, religion, marital status, pregnancy, age, disability, trade union membership and non-membership, and so on. Other statutes place duties on employers and employees concerning training, superannuation, workers' compensation and occupational health and safety. Statutory regimes exist in all of our labour law jurisdictions where employees who have been unfairly dismissed may seek reinstatement and/or compensation.

In this century, Australia has been the main arena in the western world for the operation of permanent industrial relations tribunals exercising powers of compulsory conciliation and arbitration. These tribunals have been used by the nation to bring about industrial peace via awards and collective agreements establishing fair and reasonable wages and working conditions. Pursuant to these tribunal rulings, employers are bound to comply with the terms and conditions of employment contained in the awards which cover their industries. In fact, it is not permissible to contract with employees for rates of pay or terms and conditions of employment which are below those specified in relevant awards. Employers, trade unions and employees are also bound by the provisions of collective agreements which are enforceable because they have been certified by the industrial relations tribunals.

What is of interest in our present context is that the terms and conditions of employment which are specified in awards and collective agreements usually concern only wage rates, allowances, hours of work, various forms of leave (such as annual leave, family leave and sick leave) and some aspects of the performance of the job. Few awards or collective agreements — and this is crucial to our discussion — seek to qualify the employees' duties of obedience, of good faith and fidelity and of mutual trust and confidence. Some awards merely restate these duties by safeguarding the right of the employer 'to dismiss an employee without notice for refusal of duty, malingering, inefficiency, neglect of duty or misconduct'. The scope and operation of these employee duties are left to the express and implied terms of employment contracts.

Reading between the lines

Earlier this century, it was usually the case that the terms and conditions of the employment contract — especially for factory jobs
— were not written down. These days, however — especially in
professional and staff employment — employees sign written contracts of employment and when many of these contracts are examined, it is often the case that little is said about obedience, good
faith and fidelity and mutual trust and confidence.

How then do these obligations become binding on employees?
In fact the judges have held that these duties are implied terms in
all employment contracts by force of law. Unless overridden by
express contractual terms, all contracts of employment require
employees to obey all lawful and reasonable orders; to work with
care and diligence; to act with good faith and fidelity; and to
maintain mutual trust and confidence between employer and
employee.

Implied terms are not static and may be added to or modified
by the judges. The adoption of the implied term of mutual trust
and confidence by the House of Lords in the *Malik Case* is a recent
illustration of this phenomenon. The courts have also held that
customs and practices in a particular trade, provided they are uni-
versal, will be implied by force of custom into those employment
contracts. Terms will also be implied which are necessary to the
operation of the business, and in legal parlance it is said that terms
will be implied which give business efficacy to the contract. My
focus is upon those implied terms concerning obedience, good
faith and fidelity and mutual trust and confidence, as the legal
interpretation of their scope have enhanced employer controls in
the 1990s.

4 | EMPLOYER CONTROLS OVER THE STANDARD EMPLOYEE

In a 1990 article, Hugh Collins contrasted what he called 'time-service' contracts with 'task-performance' contracts. For Collins, it was not the case that all contracts of employment could be easily fitted into either of these categories: rather, this classificatory mechanism could be adopted to enable a better understanding of the operations of the modern contract of employment. I shall use Collins' classifications to show how employer controls have increased in recent times.

Serving time and performing tasks

The time-service contract grew out of the English factory system because, especially in the 19th century, employers required employees en masse to operate machines for fixed hours each day. Most work was of a manual nature, and the new machines required the performance of precise yet repetitive tasks. In order that assembly line mechanisms could operate efficiently, it was essential for employers to have strong control over the workers during their set hours of work. Once the work day was at an end, the employer did not need to bother about what these operators did in their spare time, provided it did not diminish their capacity to perform the work. The out-of-hours opinions, hobbies and odd jobs of these employees were of little interest to their employers. The time-service contract spread from factories to shops and to low-level clerical employment. I shall call this type of employment 'standard employment' because it fits well into the early 20th century Australian paradigm of eight hours work, eight hours sleep and eight hours play.

Many employees currently work pursuant to time-service contracts, and in fact for a majority of Australians their employment can, to a greater or lesser extent, be fitted into the time service and standard employment models. Employees who work in factories, garages or in shopping centres, or who undertake defined tasks in hospitals and in clerical employment are most likely employed pursuant to time-service contracts.

On the other hand, the task-performance contract belongs to the service industries of the late 20th century. Of course, there have been task-performance contracts in the past, but for my purposes they fit the new style of corporate employment. The essence of this kind of contract is that it focuses upon performance of tasks and not on hours of work which may be required to complete the job, and so the dividing line between working hours and home hours is more flexible and employer control of out-of-hours activities has increased. Professional employees as well as an increasing number of employees below the professional ranks are finding themselves on task-performance contracts.

When employers focused upon service within working time, they were preoccupied with their controls during working hours. But as more and more employers have turned their attention to employee performance of tasks, actual working time has become less significant. It is not surprising that the performance of tasks is superseding time-controlled employment. After all, given the new computer-driven technologies, employees now have broad discretions on how any given task is to be completed, and so employment based upon rigid controls makes less sense. I predict that early in the next century more than half of employment in Australia will be task-performance driven. This has implications for the democratic structure of our society, as employees lose control over their private lives.

Controlling the standard employee

My focus in this chapter is upon the control which the law gives to employers of standard employees whose terms and conditions of work are usually governed by time-service contracts. The levers which operate these controls are the duties of obedience and of good faith and fidelity which are crucial implied terms of the common law contract of employment. Therefore, the best way of determining the boundaries of these controls is to examine the case law on them.

In its legal sense, obedience covers far more than merely obeying lawful and reasonable orders because it encompasses misconduct which embraces acts which constitute a breach of, or are inconsistent with, the performance of the employment contract. As the High Court made clear in the 1924 *Adami Case*, to warrant immediate dismissal, acts constituting misconduct must be of such a character that they show an intention by the employee to no longer be bound by the obligations of the employment contract. In other words, it is only serious acts of misconduct which courts will regard as amounting to repudiation of the employment contract by the employee. In legal terms, where the employee repudiates the contract, the employer may elect either to disregard the repudiatory act and continue with the contract, or to accept the repudiation and end the contractual relationship. This employer election to terminate is known as summary dismissal.

Good faith and fidelity is a duty of wide importance which covers employee service and loyalty to the employer. It requires the employee not to act contrary to the interests of the business of the employer and at all times to act in the interests of the enterprise. In the 1933 High Court decision of *Blyth Chemicals Ltd v Bushnell*, the High Court laid down a definition of this duty which has been accepted as definitive in subsequent Australian cases. In the view of justices Dixon and McTiernan, for conduct to warrant summary dismissal, it had to be '[c]onduct which in respect of important matters is incompatible with the fulfilment of an employee's duty, or involves an opposition, or conflict between his [sic] interest and his duty to his employer, or impedes the faithful performance of his obligations, or is destructive of the necessary confidence between employer and employee'. It can be seen that the duty of good faith and fidelity is broad in character, and its scope can be judicially expanded or contracted depending upon the view of the judge.

It cannot be too strongly stressed that there are no hard and fast demarcation lines between the general duties which are placed upon employees. For example, a persistent lateness in arriving for work could be construed as amounting to misconduct in breach of the duty of obedience, as breaking the duty of fidelity, or as breaching the employee obligation to maintain mutual trust and confidence with the employer. In my analysis, I shall classify acts of general misconduct under the duty of obedience, and shall confine breaches of good faith and fidelity to actions in opposition to, or in conflict with, the interests of the employer's business.

The cases which I shall discuss in the remainder of this book are taken from diverse areas of labour law, and this means that they lack a common approach in determining in what circumstances an employee will be in breach of her or his contractual duties. Some of the decisions come from the public sector where many aspects of employment are governed by statutory regimes which often oust the common law in the areas of demotion, suspension and termination. Other decisions have been handed down by industrial relations tribunals and courts pursuant to federal and State unfair dismissal schemes. Here, the question is often only whether the termination was unfair, and in these circumstances the contractual aspects of the employment are secondary. On the other hand, several decisions concern actions for breach of contract in the ordinary courts and in these cases there is detailed analysis of the common law contractual rules. Nevertheless, I have sought to extrapolate from these decisions the circumstances and occasions when employees will have breached their duties at law.

Obedience and misconduct

While in the past it was true that employees were required to obey all lawful orders given by their employers, it is clear that now employees are bound only to obey all lawful and reasonable orders. A recent decision covering out-of-hours work in standard employment is the *Pastry Cooks Employees' Case* which was decided by the Industrial Commission of New South Wales in 1990. In this case, a driver who had completed his deliveries of pastry goods was asked by his employer to make another delivery to a customer. In the past, drivers had agreed to make deliveries after their shifts had ended, but in this instance, the driver refused and was dismissed. In subsequent unfair dismissal proceedings he was reinstated because it was held that under his contract of employment he could not be compelled to make a late delivery. Leaving aside issues of overtime, he could not be lawfully ordered under his contract of employment to do work outside working hours. This decision typifies the sharp dividing line between working time and home time which still exists in time-service contracts.

The judicial decisions concerning misconduct in standard employment give us a clearer idea of the rather limited controls which employers have over activities engaged in out of working hours. It is obvious that not all acts which can be characterised as disobedient, criminal or immoral will amount to an employee breach of contract giving the employer the right to immediately terminate. Out-of-hours acts are held to be misconduct warranting summary dismissal only where they have a relevant connection with employment. They must either be of such a nature as to be inconsistent with future performance, or they must constitute behaviour which breaches the good faith and fidelity duty. It is clear that acts of general misbehaviour such as drunkenness and assaults committed out of hours will only amount to serious breaches of duty warranting termination where they have a relevant connection with employment. Two typical examples which I have drawn from the case law on unfair termination will suffice to make this point. In the *Transfield Case* of 1974 which came before the New South Wales Industrial Commission, it appeared that an employee who was a union delegate had a dispute on a construction site with a foreman. In the evening, the employee assaulted the foreman at a hotel where it was habitual for the workers to drink. It was held that the assault constituted misconduct warranting summary dismissal because it undermined the authority of the foreman and was inconsistent with future performance by the employee. Similarly, in the *Richards Case* which was decided in 1993 by the Western Australian Industrial Relations Commission, an employee who assaulted an industrial officer of the employing corporation at a football club's New Year's Eve party was held to have been properly dismissed. The employee had previously suffered a reprimand after the industrial officer had instituted an inquiry and this assault was seen to have been an attack upon the industrial officer's authority.

The response to criminal activities is a more interesting aspect of the limited controls which employers have over their standard employees. For a criminal offence to constitute misconduct leading to summary dismissal, it must either be clear that the employee can no longer, or is unwilling, to continue work performance, or that the offence breaches the employee's duty of good faith and fidelity. Where employees are performing menial tasks away from contact with the public, many out-of-hours crimes — unless the employee suffers imprisonment — will be irrelevant to future employee performance or to breaches of good faith. The 1938 High Court decision of *Commissioner for Railways v O'Donnell* is instructive here. O'Donnell was a junior porter in the New South Wales Railways, and he was charged with manslaughter because it was alleged he had assisted in the procurement of an illegal abortion where the woman had died. He explained to his superiors that he would be unavailable for work for several days and requested annual leave, however his employer, acting pursuant to statutory powers, suspended him for misconduct. After his subsequent acquittal, he brought an action for his wages arguing that his suspension had been unlawful. The High Court agreed with the employee's claim, holding that a charge of manslaughter unconnected with his employment did not constitute misconduct. Similarly, a conviction for drunk driving will not usually affect the performance of work or show a lack of fidelity by a factory hand. On the other hand, the same conviction could, depending upon all of the circumstances, lead to the summary termination of a bus driver.

Of course, there are instances where criminal offences are relevant to the continuation of employment, even for low or middle-ranking employees. A useful example is the 1995 *Hussein* decision where a middle-ranking employee of a bank was terminated because he had been convicted of credit card fraud. In subsequent unfair dismissal proceedings, the Industrial Relations Court of Australia held that the termination was justified because financial dishonesty prevented the employee from performing trustworthy financial employment with the bank.

Out-of-hours conduct which can be characterised as immoral raises interesting questions. In the past, when moral codes were tighter, judges were inclined to take a strict view of human lapses. In more recent times, however, society's moral code has loosened and this has made current judges more cautious in holding that immoral conduct will justify immediate dismissal. Reported decisions on immoral behaviour of standard employees are rare, but for an improper act to warrant dismissal it must diminish the capacity of the employee to perform the employment. Where employees are placed in positions of trust, such as police officers and school teachers, they are subject to stricter moral controls because even out-of-hours activities may be regarded as inconsistent with their future employment. It is difficult to separate out decisions dealing with standard employees from those concerning persons who occupy higher positions. In this chapter, however, the two following examples will suffice.

In an atypical decision in 1963 in *Henry v Ryan*, it was held by the Supreme Court of Tasmania that the termination of a police officer was justified when he was discovered in the grounds of a girl's school wearing only his underpants. Given the powers and status of police, it was held that this type of conduct was inconsistent with his future employment as a police officer.

In the unusual 1982 case of *Wall v Westcott* which dealt with a middle-ranking employee in the private sector, it was held that an employee in a small country town who had had an affair with the employer's wife was guilty of misconduct warranting summary termination. As the judge in the Industrial Commission of New South Wales put it, the deliberate affront to the employer was inconsistent with future service.

Good faith and fidelity

Here, I wish to focus upon the aspect of good faith and fidelity which requires employees not to act against the business interests of their employer. There are few decisions which deal with situations where standard employees undertake outside activities which can be regarded as opposing the interests of the employer's business. This is not surprising as most standard employees usually do not have the occasion or opportunity to engage in such conduct.

The standard precedent in this area is the 1946 decision of the English Court of Appeal in *Hivac Ltd v Park Royal Scientific Instruments Ltd*. The Hivac Company manufactured miniature valves for hearing aids and they also produced small valves for the military in World War II. Two of its employees, who were husband and wife, together with three other employees, began secretly on weekends to assemble valves for the Park Royal Company, a competitor of Hivac. Given the wartime restrictions on terminating employees which were still in force, Hivac sought and obtained an injunction precluding Park Royal from employing Hivac employees to undertake this type of assembling work. Although the Hivac employees were manual workers, they did possess rather specialised knowledge on the assembling process for making these valves and their work did greatly assist Park Royal. The judges concluded that the employees did know that their work for the Park Royal Company was injurious to their employer and, in part, that was why they kept it secret from Hivac. In these circumstances, the Court of Appeal was prepared to issue the injunction. In his judgment, Lord Greene said that usually it was no business of the employer what the ordinary employee did in her or his spare time, but the present circumstances were highly unusual. But he also said that higher ranking employees did owe a broader duty of good faith and fidelity. He illustrated this position by arguing that for a solicitor's clerk to work for another law firm on Sundays would be a breach of the duty because this type of out-of-hours work conflicted with her or his employment in the legal profession.

There is no Australian decision similar to the *Hivac Case*, but the 1933 High Court decision of *Blyth Chemicals Ltd v Bushnell* deserves comment. Bushnell was employed as a manager by Jacobs Pty Ltd which was under the control of Blyth Chemicals. Subsequently, Bushnell — in his spare time — became the Managing Director of another company which could potentially compete with Blyth Chemicals. After being summarily dismissed, Bushnell successfully brought a common law action for wrongful dismissal. In the view of the High Court judges, there was no evidence that Bushnell had breached the duty of good faith and fidelity. While the company of which he had become Managing Director had the potential to compete with Blyth Chemicals, it had not done so. Furthermore, there was no evidence of any impropriety by Bushnell. This decision shows that breach of good faith and fidelity requires acts which are either in competition with, or which are in direct opposition to the employer's business.

I can find only one Australian precedent dealing with the freedom of speech of a time-service contract employee and this is the 1946 decision of the Commonwealth Court of Conciliation and Arbitration in the *Cockatoo Docks Case*. An employee who wrote an article in a Labor Party newspaper which was critical of his employer was terminated and, in a very brief judgment, the Court upheld this dismissal. It appears that the judge must have regarded this conduct as a breach of the duty of good faith and fidelity as the article was seen as being in direct opposition to the interests of the employer's business. I surmise that the upholding of the dismissal may have been related to left-wing agitation in the cold war climate of that time. In present day Australia, I suggest, this decision would not be followed with respect to standard employees.

In conclusion, it does appear that the controls which employers have over the out-of-hours activities of standard employees are limited. Unless the conduct possesses a relevant connection with the employment because it is inconsistent with future performance or it is clearly contrary to business interests, it is not the concern of the employer.

5 | THE RISE OF PROFESSIONAL AND STAFF EMPLOYMENT

For most of my adult life, my occupation has been that of an academic lawyer who researches the law and teaches it to students. I am fortunate to have a job which I enjoy and find fulfilling, however one of the features of my employment which I share with a majority of professional and staff employees is that I have no daily knock-off time. If tomorrow's lecture necessitates work at home until late in the evening, well that is just part of my work. The computer-driven technology about which I wrote in Chapter 2, facilitates my evening and weekend work because it brings my office documents and library materials right inside our home. In fact, at present I appear to do more of my research work — which requires long pre-dawn periods of quiet — at home rather than in my office.

Unlike most professional and staff employees, we academics do receive a broad range of tangible and intangible rewards for our work and, by the standards of most workers and of a majority of professional employees, we are well remunerated. For many of us, there is a relatively high level of employment security, and there is some flexibility as to when we must attend at our institutions, making family life easier. This flexibility needs to be weighed up against the disadvantages of allowing work to intrude into our home lives.

In this chapter, I shall further examine the nature of professional and staff employment as well as the increased use of written contracts of employment.

Professional employment

In the late 20th century there has been a mushrooming of new professions and a high level of professional people employed by firms, governments and corporations. Just how and when a skill becomes a profession is a complex question, but it is clear that the varieties of professions have increased and that very many people consider themselves to be employed in a professional capacity. Journalists, social workers, school teachers, airline pilots, human resource managers, business executives, university academics, psychologists, therapists, laboratory technicians and information technology specialists usually refer to their callings as professions. Within this expanding group I include the growing number of para-professionals, such as paralegals and paramedics, who assist professionals with their work. Although many professionals are sole practitioners, self-employed consultants or partners in firms, the majority of professionals and para-professionals are employees at law employed mainly by professional firms, hospitals, teaching institutions, corporations, Federal Government, and State and Local Governments.

The law has always treated professional occupations differently to others by placing higher duties upon them. The clearest statement of the nature of professional employment which I can find is in the 1986 *Sim* decision, which was handed down by Scott J sitting in the English Divisional Court. The case was concerned with when and under what circumstances secondary school teachers could be compelled to take extra classes when any of their colleagues were absent. Scott J made the following comments on the duties of professional employees. He said:

> ... A teacher could not excuse a failure to be properly prepared for a class, or a failure to mark school work within a reasonable time after it had been done, by pointing out, correct though the observation might be, that he or she had not had time within school hours to do the work. It is, perhaps, one of the hallmarks of professional employment, as opposed to employment in non-professional capacities, that professionals are employed to provide a particular service and have a contractual obligation to do so properly. A worker in a car factory or shop may clock off at 5:30 pm or, perhaps, work late on an overtime basis. An employed professional does not usually have an overtime option. He [sic] is employed to provide a particular service to proper professional standards. His contract may require his attendance in an office or other place of work for particular hours but his contractual obligations are not necessarily limited to work done within those hours.

This judicial pronouncement gives contractual backing to the reality that professional employees have legal obligations to complete tasks in accordance with professional standards, even if this requires extra work beyond their contractual hours of employment, whether performed at the office or at home on evenings or during weekends. Professional employees are expected to work long hours either at home or in the office and it is common these days to work a 50 and even a 55-hour week. These expectations come both from the employer and through peer pressure from colleagues. These long hours take away family and leisure time and limit the capacity of professional employees to participate in community activities.

Staff employment

Another feature of late 20th century corporate life is the growing phenomenon of staff employment — that is, employees (other than professionals) who enter into express contractual arrangements where, for financial and other rewards, employers impose upon them duties similar to those which the common law employment contract places upon professional employees. I have called them 'staff employees' because their corporate employers regard them as members of their staff whose primary loyalty is to the employer. It is usual for workers who are offered the status of staff employment to be dealt with on an individual rather than a collective basis and, in return for loyalty to the corporation, they usually agree to individual salary arrangements via a performance appraisal mechanism. Many of their entitlements, such as leave arrangements, are spelled out in corporate policies which are expressly incorporated into their staff employment contracts. Staff employees are obviously employed pursuant to task-performance contracts and, when appraised, the focus is upon the nature and quality of completed tasks. The labour law deregulation in the 1990s, coupled with the fall in trade union membership, has opened up a space which is being filled by individual employment arrangements including staff employment. In the late 1990s, the fastest growing form of employee regulation is the common law contract of employment which is often underpinned by safety net awards, but which is not supplemented by collective agreements.

As staff employment is usually created by express contractual provisions emphasising individual achievement and corporate loyalty, the best method of understanding this form of employment is to examine some of these contractual provisions. A useful example is the standard contract which CRA (now Rio Tinto) offered to the employees at its Weipa aluminium smelter in northern Queensland. (I have decided to use this standard contract because it is within the public domain.) It was reproduced in the 1996 *Australian Manufacturing Workers' Union Case* which came before the Australian Industrial Relations Commission when that tribunal sought to settle the dispute at Weipa over the use of individual contracts. The focus of the Weipa staff contract is on corporate loyalty for it states: 'It is a condition of your employment that you do not undertake any paid or unpaid activity which is damaging to the interests of the Company.' As would be expected, the contract is centred upon individual performance which is task-oriented. It says: 'While the normal working week is 40 hours, you will be required to work such reasonable time as is necessary to perform your duties.' Salary arrangements are on an individual basis which are reviewed through an appraisal mechanism, and other employee benefits are significant. The contract also seeks to deal with conflicts between corporate loyalty and the private concerns of staff employees. Two significant paragraphs provide:

> It is your responsibility to raise any potential conflicts of interest with your superintendent and you will be informed if the activities are judged to be in conflict with the Company's interests.
> Involvement in social, sporting, community, welfare, religious, artistic and political activities would not normally conflict with Company interests.

While membership of a football club clearly would not raise a conflict of interests issue, what if a staff employee were to join an environmental organisation which was opposed to the opening up of a new mine by the employer? A strong argument could be mounted that membership of the environmental body could amount to breach of the employment contract warranting summary termination. This shows the breadth of some express contractual provisions which govern significant numbers of staff employees.

Putting it in writing

Up until the recent past, most employers did not require their standard and even their professional employees to sign written contracts.

It was enough for the contract to come into existence through the signing of a brief letter of acceptance because the interests of employers were safeguarded by the implied duties of obedience and good faith and fidelity. Over the decade of the 1990s however, increasing numbers of employers require their professional and staff employees to enter into lengthy written contracts which spell out appropriate behaviour and loyalty issues. This is often achieved by incorporating corporate policies and/or codes of conduct. It is usual for these codes and policies to cover not merely employee conduct and comportment, but also restrictions on employees informing the media and other outsiders about corporate activities without receiving express permission. Where the code of conduct or corporate policy is made an express term of the employment contract, then breach of the code or policy is breach of the contract.

It does appear that the use of codes of conduct and corporate policies in contracts are on the increase, especially in the public sector where State Governments, municipal governments and their agencies have sought to restrict employee comment through the use of codes of conduct. A useful example is the code of conduct which the Victorian Public Service Commissioner has established for Victorian public sector employees. After reminding Victorian public servants of statutory restrictions which limit political comment, the code of conduct states:

> There are additional circumstances in which public comment is inappropriate unless specifically authorised by your chief executive officer. These include circumstances where:
> * the implication that the public comment, although made in a private capacity, is in some way an official comment on government policy or programs; and
> * you are directly involved in advising or directing the implementation or administration of government policy, and the public comment would compromise your ability to do so.

Similar restrictions are placed upon teachers in Victorian government schools albeit through the use of a ministerial order.

The above passage is worded with care and, in my opinion, unnecessarily limits genuine employee free speech. After all, before making a comment a Victorian public sector employee would need to obtain the assistance of a lawyer to determine when a communication which was made in a private capacity would be in breach of the code. Otherwise the statement could be regarded as an official comment because the employee was in some direct way involved in the administration of an area of government policy and the comment would compromise the public servant in this work. There are few decisions where codes of conduct or corporate policies have played a central role in terminations, but there is little doubt that they are effective control mechanisms. These controls are explored further in the next chapter.

6 | EMPLOYER CONTROLS OVER PROFESSIONAL AND STAFF EMPLOYEES

As a university teacher throughout most of my life, I have had the opportunity to speak out and to write without fear or favour. For the vast bulk of professional employees, however, freedom of expression and of action has been more tightly circumscribed. In order to unmask the increased reach of employment law, in this chapter I shall examine the concepts of corporate image, moral behaviour, freedom of speech and employer controls upon the provision of work.

'Corporate image' refers to the recognition by the law that corporate employers may place controls upon employees to protect their image which is a necessary element of their businesses. My discussion of moral impropriety will be confined largely to out-of-hours sexual conduct, while my focus on freedom of speech will concern when and on what occasions employees may speak out about actual or supposed corporate wrongdoing.

Corporate image and corporate control

It is clear that especially in the service sector of our economy, corporate and firm image is a crucial part of competitive business. Acts of employees which can be seen to tarnish this image are arguably detrimental to the employer's business. No Australian precedents of which I am aware directly home in on the concept of corporate image, yet in some cases it hovers in the background. It is therefore a useful tool in explaining some legal decisions involving employee conduct.

In the last chapter I discussed how, for professional and staff employees, lengthy written contracts have displaced more informal arrangements. I believe that these contracts incorporate policies and/or codes of conduct in order to heighten and to legally formalise corporate image as a control mechanism.

Employee dress and grooming — leaving aside matters of decency and safety — has been traditionally regarded as a matter for individual employees and this is why the 1982 Federal Court decision in the *Hart Case* is of such interest. In this matter, Telecom (now known as Telstra) ordered one of its senior technical officers, who performed clerical duties out of the sight of the general public, to refrain from wearing a kaftan and thongs to work. After the officer was fined by a disciplinary board, he sought judicial review of the decision of the board in the Federal Court of Australia. Speaking for the Full Court majority, Fox J with whom Sheppard J concurred, upheld the decision of the board stating that the employer's direction on this matter of dress to the officer was lawful and reasonable. It does appear that these judges focused too heavily upon whether the order was reasonable, rather than upon whether the contract of employment contained an implied term which would justify the order. I prefer the reasoning of Smithers J at first instance and of Northropp J who was the minority judge in the Full Court. For these judges, the question was whether the contract of employment enabled the employer to make the direction. The only term which they would imply into the contract to give it business efficacy was to the effect that the employee would dress in a reasonable manner. Given that the officer did not have much contact with the general public, the wearing of a kaftan was not an unreasonable form of dress.

It does seem beyond doubt however, that if the officer had contact with the public — perhaps through visiting premises to repair telephones — all of the judges would have held that to protect its image with the public, Telecom would have possessed implied contractual powers to place tight controls upon employee dress, grooming and behaviour. I have no doubt, for example, that a legal or an accountancy firm would possess ample common law contractual powers to direct its professional employees to dress and to behave in a manner deemed appropriate by them. Firms and corporations could probably rely upon an implied term to the effect that professional employees will comport themselves in a manner which will uphold the operations and the public image of the corporation or firm.

Many corporate employers either supply or subsidise the purchase of company uniforms. Some corporate employers have written policies which cover the behaviour of employees whilst in uniform and, if made part of the contract of employment, these policies are enforceable. Given that the uniform is one of the faces of the corporation, employees whilst wearing the uniform, even when out of hours, are subject to employer discipline.

The wearing of badges and emblems has reached the courts on a couple of occasions. In the 1912 *Australian Tramways Case*, H B Higgins J sitting in the Commonwealth Court of Conciliation and Arbitration upheld the right of the employees to wear union badges on their watch chains as part of a union-organising campaign. On the other hand, in the 1977 *Boychuk Case* which came before the English Employment Appeal Tribunal, the dismissal of an audit clerk was confirmed. The employee concerned had refused to remove a badge from her clothing which contained the words 'lesbians ignite'. The Tribunal held that management possessed the discretion to order the removal of an emblem which caused distress to fellow employees and to visitors. It is difficult to state with exactness the width of managerial discretion to limit the wearing of badges and emblems by employees. Much will depend upon the operations and image of the firm, the employee's contact with clients and the general public, and the size and wording of the badge or emblem.

Would the upholding of corporate image extend to out-of-hours activities of professional and staff employees? Given the nature of professional and staff employment, I have no doubt that some out-of-hours activities could be regulated. Where employees are wearing corporate uniforms after hours, it is clear that they can be required to conduct themselves in a proper manner. It is also clear that a law firm, for example, could prohibit its professional employees from undertaking external employment which might bring the firm into disrepute, such as working as a bouncer or bartender at a nightclub.

Employers may also forbid professional and high-ranking employees from engaging in out-of-hours employment which is inconsistent with their employment. It will be recalled that in the 1946 *Hivac Case*, Lord Greene said that for a solicitor's clerk to work for an opposition firm on Sundays would be inconsistent with the primary employment. For an Australian professional or even for a staff employee to work out of hours for a competitor would, in my view, be a breach of the implied term of good faith and fidelity. Many employers — especially in the fields of sport and entertainment — protect their image by expressly providing in contracts of employment that the employee will not undertake additional paid work without the employer's permission.

One case that juxtaposes corporate image with private activity is *Rose v Telstra Corporation* which was decided by Vice President Ross of the Australian Industrial Relations Commission in late 1998. Mr Rose was employed by Telstra as a communications officer who installed and maintained telephone equipment for customers. He was based in Tamworth, New South Wales, but owing to increased work in Armidale Mr Rose agreed to go and work there for four days. Whilst there, he shared a hotel room with another Telstra employee named Mr Mitchell and both men received a travel allowance payment from Telstra. One evening after both men had been drinking in a nightclub, a scuffle between them took place in their hotel room and a window was broken. The Industrial Relations Commission found that Rose had verbally provoked Mitchell, and then Mitchell struck Rose in the chest with a piece of glass. Mitchell was subsequently convicted and imprisoned and Rose was suspended and then dismissed for improper conduct. He challenged the fairness of this termination before the Industrial Relations Commission. Vice President Ross in a thorough and detailed decision held that the termination was unfair. He said that apart from both men being employees of Telstra, the facts gave rise to no other relevant connection with the employer because the employees were off duty and neither was in his Telstra uniform. Unlike the 1974 *Transfield Case* and the 1993 *Richards* decision which were discussed in Chapter 4, here there were no supervision issues between these two employees and there was no suggestion that Rose was seeking to undermine or to threaten Mitchell because of their joint employment.

Why then did Telstra dismiss Rose for improper conduct? Possibly Telstra was concerned that this hotel room fight in a small town with subsequent court proceedings had damaged its corporate image. In 1996, Telstra adopted a code of conduct titled 'Our Company Values and Our Code of Conduct' which was mailed to all its employees. The relevant paragraph of the code said:

> We should avoid outside activity likely to affect adversely either our work or someone else's (for example, in terms of occupational health and safety), or which could discredit either ourselves or our Company, or which could conflict with the Company interests.

In the proceedings, it was not argued that the code had become part of the employment contract whereby a breach of the code would be a breach of contract and there was no suggestion in the code that a serious breach would lead to dismissal. Yet, I believe that for Telstra the code represented its behavioural standards both during and out of hours. It was, I suggest, a lapse in these standards which Telstra perceived as lessening its corporate image and which prompted the termination. With respect to corporate image, however, Vice President Ross held that there was no evidence that this employee behaviour had tarnished Telstra's good name. In conclusion, the Vice President said that:

> ... [E]mployers do not have an unfettered right to sit in judgment on the out-of-work behaviour of their employees. An employee is entitled to a private life. The circumstances in which an employee may be validly terminated because of their conduct outside work are limited. The facts of this case do not fall within those limited circumstances.

In my view, this decision is a timely reminder to employers of the limits of their controls over the out-of-hours activities of their employees. Yet, on slightly different facts the result may have been different. The code of conduct may have been broader and may have provided that breach could lead to termination, or the code could have been incorporated into the employment contract giving rise to issues of breach of contract. There could have been evidence of adverse publicity against Telstra, or the employees may have occupied higher ranks in the Telstra hierarchy. While corporate image was not considered in the circumstances of this decision, I contend that as a mechanism of control, corporate image is alive and well in Australia.

Moral behaviour and professional employees

It does appear that for professional employees — and especially those in leadership positions — moral behaviour can become an issue with respect to employment. This includes sexual behaviour and the use of alcohol and drugs.

One area where issues of moral behaviour has been significant is in the education industry where teachers have responsibility over children and young people. The most famous Australian decision on out-of-hours immoral conduct in the education industry is the 1957 *Orr* decision. In this case, a university professor who had had consensual sexual intercourse with a 19-year-old female student was held by the High Court to have committed acts of misconduct which enabled the university to summarily terminate his professorship. I venture to think that were a similar instance to come before a current court, while the facts would still give rise to misconduct, the reasons would focus more upon the image of a university as an educational institution than on whether the professor had overwhelmed the young student.

It will be recalled from the discussion of *Commissioner for Railways v O'Donnell* in Chapter 4, that for the commission of a criminal offence to warrant summary termination there must be a relevant connection between the offence and the employment. This is also the rule for professional employees, however if employees hold positions of trust or leadership, or if they are teaching or caring for young children, it is easier to show such a relevant connection. In my view, the conviction must be of such a nature as to demonstrate that the employee no longer warrants trustworthiness, leadership or the responsibility of nurturing the young. In *R v Teachers' Board*, for example, a school teacher was dismissed after being convicted for the second time of cultivating Indian hemp. Under the relevant statutory scheme, a teacher could be dismissed when guilty of disgraceful or improper conduct. In 1974 the South Australian Supreme Court upheld the decision of the Teachers' Board, stating that it was open to it to find that these convictions amounted to disgraceful or improper conduct. While reasonable minds may differ on whether the growing of marijuana is disgraceful or improper conduct, two criminal convictions for cultivation do show a clear disregard of the law by a person in a position of trust and care.

It must be appreciated that employment by religious bodies — and more especially the employment of teachers in religious schools — raises complex questions concerning the behaviour of teachers and instruction of the young in religious doctrine. It is not my intention here to deal with this matter exhaustively. Several decisions on purely private moral and sexual behaviour have arisen in religious contexts and warrant comment here because of the ordinariness of the behaviour at the centre of these cases.

The 1979 decision of the English Court of Appeal in *Jones v*

Lee is a useful starting point. Mr Jones was a head teacher of a Catholic primary school, and during his employment at the school he befriended a female teacher. These two teachers divorced their respective partners and married one another, but the woman decided to move to another school. When the authorities learned of the remarriage of Mr Jones, they dismissed him. Jones was successful before the Court of Appeal, which issued an injunction, because under the relevant procedures and legislation the teacher could not be dismissed without a prior hearing. The eventual outcome of this matter is unknown to me, but in Australia at the turn of the millennium it is my view that this private behaviour should not be regarded as the business of an educational body even if it is a religious school.

A more recent case is the 1997 decision of *Hozack v Church of Jesus Christ of Latter-Day Saints*. Ms Hozack was employed as a part-time office receptionist by the Church of Jesus Christ of Latter-Day Saints. It was an express condition of her employment that she conduct herself so as to obtain a 'temple recommend' which is an annual commendation of the behaviour of Church members which enables them to worship at the temple and be temple-worthy. It came to the attention of the Church authorities that Ms Hozack, who was separated from her husband but not divorced, was having a sexual relationship with a man. She suffered disfellowship which meant that she was no longer temple-worthy and was subsequently dismissed. Ms Hozack brought proceedings for unfair termination which came before Madgwick J in the Federal Court of Australia.

In relation to religious schools and institutions, federal termination law, which is now to be found in the *Workplace Relations Act 1996,* does give churches some latitude to dismiss employees on grounds including religion, gender, sexual preference and marital status, provided the termination is in good faith to avoid injury to the religious susceptibilities of the members of the church. Madgwick J held that while it was open to the Church to terminate Ms Hozack on the grounds of religion to protect the religious susceptibilities of its members, this did not mean that the Church could avoid the general termination provisions which require fairness. This case was decided under the now repealed 1993 termination laws where employers were required to show that they had a valid reason for termination based on operational requirements, and so the judgment operates within this framework. For Madgwick J, however, this termination could not be upheld as valid because Ms Hozack was employed in a low-level position where she was not expected to give leadership and where her work was not of a religious nature. In my view, Madgwick J correctly applied the law.

Two recent decisions discuss controls over out-of-hours conduct where the employer argued that the behaviour amounted to sexual harassment. The first is the 1996 Federal Court of Australia decision in *McManus v Scott-Charlton*, while the second, called *Applicant v Respondent*, was decided by the Australian Industrial Relations Commission in early 1999. In *McManus v Scott-Charlton*, Mr McManus was a clerical employee in the Australian public service and his superiors ordered him to refrain from making out-of-hours telephone calls which were unwelcome and sexually harassing, to the home of a woman who was a fellow employee. In judicial review proceedings before Finn J in the Federal Court, McManus challenged the legality of the order. The statutory scheme of employment for federal public servants is not my concern in this context. The importance of this decision is that Finn J, in a careful and measured judgment, upheld the order. Apart from being fellow workers, McManus and the woman had never had any other contact; the out-of-hours phone calls did amount to sexual harassment and this conduct did have adverse effects upon the workplace. Finn J was ' ... [M]indful of the caution that should be exercised when any extension is made to the supervision allowed an employer over the private activities of an employee.' Yet, in these circumstances, the common law contract of employment did permit this type of direction. Finn J put the matter thus:

> ... [I]t is lawful for an employer to give an employee a direction to prevent the repetition of privately engaged-in sexual harassment of a co-employee where:
>
> (i) that harassment can reasonably be said to be a consequence of the relationship of the parties as co-employees (that is, it is employment-related); and;
>
> (ii) the harassment has had and continues to have substantial and adverse effects on workplace relations, workplace performance and/or the

'efficient, equitable and proper conduct' ... of the employer's business because of the proximity of the harasser and the harassed person in the workplace.

In *Applicant v Respondent*, the applicant who was employed as an international flight attendant by the respondent airline, challenged his termination asserting that it was unfair. The applicant flew as part of a cabin crew to a foreign destination where they went off duty and several went drinking with members of another crew of flight attendants which included the complainant. During the evening, much alcohol was consumed and what was described as 'some skylarking' took place. In the early hours of the morning when the complainant was sick, the applicant escorted her to her hotel room, wiped vomit from her hair, assisted her to undress down to her underpants and helped her get into bed. The applicant stated that the complainant asked him to stay, however he left to continue drinking but later returned. Upon his return, the applicant undressed and climbed into the complainant's bed where heavy petting and oral sex took place. The complainant stated that when she awoke she found the applicant in bed beside her, but she remembered little about the nocturnal events in her hotel room. She made a complaint to the respondent airline which, after conducting an investigation, dismissed the applicant.

It was the view of the respondent airline that the conduct of the applicant amounted to sexual harassment and that it breached its sexual harassment policy which had been distributed to all employees. Furthermore, the conduct was employee-related because the applicant and complainant were in the foreign destination owing to their employment, and because their hotel accommodation was paid for by the airline. For the Deputy President, it was significant that the conduct took place when the applicant and the complainant were off duty in the privacy of a hotel room. After observing the witnesses, the Deputy President found that in all of the circumstances the termination was unfair. The Full Bench, which did not see the witnesses, upheld the reinstatement order.

In my view, the Tribunal handed down a lenient decision because the respondent airline had a strong case that the complained of conduct was employment-related and that such behaviour did cause friction between fellow employees who are required to cooperate together as flight attendants.

Finally, in this discussion of moral conduct, I shall comment upon a recent Federal Court case dealing with the drug testing of employees. While drug testing occurs in working hours, it does raise questions about employer controls over the private moral behaviour of employees, especially where drug taking occurs out of hours and where it does not impact upon employment. The legality of drug testing orders arose in the 1997 Federal Court of Australia decision in *Anderson v Sullivan*. Mr Anderson, who was a member of the Australian Federal Police, was ordered by superiors to provide a urine sample because of suspicion that he had been taking drugs. He judicially challenged the legality of this order in the Federal Court before Finn J. The judge held the order could not be wholly justified under the legislative scheme relating to this police force. But the Commissioner of Police possessed the general administration and control of the Force and had developed a policy where drug testing of police was permissible upon reasonable suspicion of drug use. In the view of Finn J, the Commissioner could delegate the power to give this type of order. At common law, Anderson was required to obey all lawful and reasonable orders. Finn J, in a careful analysis of the legal boundaries, was prepared to hold the order lawful and reasonable, but only with respect to the testing of urine when there was evidence of reasonable suspicion of drug taking. In my view, the order to produce a urine sample for the purpose of testing for drug use is an invasive procedure and requires more than general enabling words to justify it. These matters are best dealt with by statutory provisions as is the case with the New South Wales police.

Although this decision certainly does not justify drug testing beyond the police, an increasing number of employers are establishing drug testing procedures which are usually set out in collective agreements and occasionally as express terms of employment contracts.

Freedom to speak out

The capacities of employees to engage in free speech very much depend upon their employers. As I showed in Chapter 4, the Victorian Public Service Code of Conduct does seek to limit the freedom of speech of Victorian public servants. In that same chapter, I also examined the CRA staff employment contract and argued that, for an employee to join an environmental organisation which was opposed to the Corporation opening up a mine, would arguably amount to a breach of contract. Although a majority of private sector employees are free to speak out on political, environmental and safety matters, clashes can and do occur with employers when out-of-hours actions are perceived as being in opposition to the interests of the corporation, particularly where the employee is making comment upon the activities of the corporation or firm. Employees of the 1990s increasingly are well educated, possess much specialised knowledge and are politically aware and so are in a better position to speak out about what is going on in their place of work. In fact, one feature of the 1990s has been the enactment in several of the States — but not at federal level — of whistleblowers protection legislation which seeks to protect from termination and victimisation employees who speak out about corrupt or maladministrative practices in government. There is no whistleblowers protective legislation for the private sector but, given the number of public services which have been privatised, there are growing reasons to extend it into some areas of private employment.

As yet, few Australian decisions have concerned speaking out in the private sector, but this issue is likely to be of some significance in the coming years. An interesting case is that of *Davis v Nokia Telecommunications,* which was decided by the Industrial Relations Court of Australia in 1996. Mr Davis was a warehouse controller with Nokia (which supplies and repairs telecommunications equipment), however, he spent a significant amount of his time handling the processing of repairs. Nokia decided to use a computer system called Scala to keep records on repairs and Davis was directed to implement this system. He refused, asserting that Scala could not do the job adequately, and he was dismissed. In the view of the Court, Davis was correct in asserting that there were problems over the way the system handled repair prices from different Nokia localities and therefore his termination was unfair. Interestingly, much of the evidence before the Court on the effectiveness of Scala was contained in printed out email messages.

During the initial hearing of this matter before Judicial Registrar Patch, Davis sent two faxes to the President of Nokia in Finland making serious allegations about several Nokia management staff in Australia. As Davis would not be working closely with any of the staff named in the faxes, the Judicial Registrar ordered reinstatement. On Review, Wilcox CJ confirmed the reinstatement order. In relation to the two faxes to the President of Nokia, Wilcox CJ said:

> An employee of a company is entitled to draw the attention of a senior officer of the company to matters that the employee perceives to be irregular or poorly handled, without thereby being treated as unfit for continued or further employment. It is in the interests of the company itself for managers, at all levels, to accept this entitlement; otherwise junior officers will feel inhibited about calling attention to matters that ought to be investigated and perhaps rectified. It is, of course, important that the allegations be made in the right way and to the right person. It would be wrong for an employee to make public allegations damaging to the employer's business and reputation; at least, not unless the employee was satisfied they were accurate and there was an overriding public duty to do so. But Mr Davis did not make his allegations public. He made them to the person who was best placed to investigate the position and take appropriate action.

It is clear that employees cannot make external statements damaging to their employer's business unless the making of the statements is in the public interest, but when and on what occasions will employees be able to speak freely? The 1949 New South Wales Supreme Court decision of *Associated Dominions Assurance Society v Andrew* shows that where employees honestly report illegalities to the proper authorities, they will not breach good faith and fidelity. In this case, the Assurance Society's accountant wrote to a government department and spoke to a Member of Parliament about some of the Society's returns which he had signed but which he believed had been subsequently altered. In legal proceedings, the Supreme Court held that there was insufficient evidence to warrant summary dismissal. Jordan CJ said that where an employee innocently became a party to an employer breach of law:

> ... [T]he employee's duty as a citizen and his [sic] interest in exculpating himself from a possible charge of being an accomplice, might well override any duty he would otherwise owe to his employer not to disclose to outsiders details of his employer's business.

When will it be in the public interest for employees to speak out about corporate wrongdoing to the media? Two English decisions are apposite here. In *Initial Services Ltd v Putterill*, Mr Putterill was the sales manager of Initial Services Ltd which laundered towels for gymnasiums and sports venues. Putterill resigned and disclosed to the *Daily Mail* newspaper that Initial Services and other launderers had entered into an arrangement to keep up prices contrary to the English equivalent of our *Trade Practices Act*. After the *Daily Mail* published these allegations, the company brought proceedings against it and Putterill, asserting that Putterill had disclosed confidential information and that the newspaper was a party to the disclosure. In their defence, Putterill and the newspaper asserted that disclosure was in the public interest. In proceedings which came before the English Court of Appeal in 1967, the Court refused to disallow the defence, holding that although the allegations were not of criminal wrongdoing, the public interest warranted disclosure of possible breaches of the competition laws. Lord Denning adopted the words of Vice Chancellor Wood as stated in the 1856 *Gartside Case* that 'There is no confidence as to the disclosure of iniquity.' In other words, it was in the public interest to disclose serious employer misconduct.

More recently, the English Court of Appeal adopted a broader approach in the 1984 decision of *Lion Laboratories v Evans*. The plaintiff Corporation — Lion Laboratories — manufactured and sold breathalyser machines which are known in the United Kingdom as intoximeters and these machines were used by the police for measuring alcohol intoxication by drivers. In early 1984, Evans and Smith, who were two senior technicians of the plaintiff company, resigned their positions and took with them documentary information on the intoximeter which was obtained by the *Daily Express* newspaper. The documents appeared to show that the intoximeter was prone to great error and, if substantiated, would affect the convictions of many drivers who had been tested and found to have an alcohol level above the prescribed limit. The English Court of Appeal discharged a first instance injunction, holding that although there was no proven employer misconduct, given the possible effects on the convictions of drivers, the public interest in disclosure outweighed the public interest in maintaining confidences. The law on this point is not completely settled in Australia because it is unclear whether serious employer misconduct is a prerequisite to public interest disclosures or, whether without misconduct, the public interest may justify some disclosures. In my view, however, it does appear that where an employee (or more likely a former employee) disclosed to the media that a manufactured pharmaceutical product was medically dangerous, an Australian court would allow disclosure in the public interest despite the absence of employer transgressions. I am unaware of any recent Australian decisions where existing employees have justified disclosures of information in the public interest: no doubt this is because any existing employee who did disclose would no longer have a future in the employing enterprise.

Leaving aside disclosures in the public interest, it is clear that under the existing law employee external comment about the operations of the employer is still very limited. A decision which illustrates this limitation is the 1993 holding by the Supreme Court of Victoria in *Lane v Fasciale*. Mr Lane was the Principal of a Catholic girl's college which the Parish Council had decided to close. Lane attended a public meeting and spoke out against the closure. He was then ordered by the employing priest to refrain from further public comment on this matter. After refusing to comply he was terminated, but his court action for wrongful dismissal failed. While in the view of the judge a teacher has the right to speak out about issues concerning the welfare of students, once he had been directed to refrain from further comment because the closure decision had been finalised, subsequent statements were breaches of the duty of good faith and fidelity.

Employer controls over the provision of work

While there has been an increase in the breadth of the duties which employees owe to their employers and, while in areas like occupational health and safety increased obligations have been placed upon employers, in other areas of employer obligations the law is still rather old-fashioned. For example, under the existing case law, so long as employers pay employees their wages, there is no duty upon them to provide work, other than in the case of entertainers and sports persons. In fact, the law is still as it was in 1940 when in the *Collier Case* Asquith J could say:

It is true that a contract of employment does not necessarily, or perhaps normally, oblige the master to provide the servant with work. Provided I pay my cook her [sic] wages regularly she cannot complain if I choose to take any or all of my meals out.

A useful illustration of the present law is the 1981 Federal Court of Australia decision in *Mann v Capital Territory Health Commission*. In 1974, Dr Mann, an experienced general surgeon, accepted an offer of employment from the Canberra Hospitals Management Board which later became the Capital Territory Health Commission. In that year, the Medicare health scheme was established whereby all Australians could receive free medical attention, and the Board had decided that it would employ salaried (rather than consultant) surgeons to perform surgery in its hospitals. When negotiating his acceptance, Dr Mann sought assurances that he would receive sufficient surgery to maintain and to enhance his surgical skills. In 1976, however, some time after a change of government, it was decided that no longer would Medicare surgical work in the hospitals be given solely to salaried surgeons but would be shared between them and the private specialists. While Dr Mann's salary remained unchanged, he found that he was receiving insufficient surgical work to maintain his skill levels.

In an action which began in the Supreme Court of the Australian Capital Territory, Dr Mann asserted that the Board and its successor body had breached a term in his employment contract that he would be furnished with suitable and sufficient surgical work for a specialist with his seniority. In the Federal Court, however, Fox and Kelly JJ held that no such term was to be implied into the contract and accordingly the action failed. In his dissent, Sheppard J held in reliance on the written and oral evidence of the negotiations that the contract did contain an express term that Dr Mann would receive sufficient surgery and that the Board was guilty of breach of contract. While the circumstances which faced Dr Mann were perhaps atypical, in my view he had a strong case because he had been given tenure until he reached 65 years of age and he required sufficient work to retain his surgical skills.

7 | RESTORING THE BALANCE

This book aims to emphasise that employer controls on the private and out-of-hours activities of professional and staff employees have increased over the last 25 years. The use of lengthy written contracts which often incorporate policies and/or codes of conduct, coupled with the concept of corporate image, have lead to a tightening of employer controls until they are somewhat akin to those which 18th century masters had over their servants. In Chapter 2, I examined changes in the nature of work, the rise of computer-driven technologies and the globalisation of the Australian economy because I believe that the employer controls on professional and staff employees must be viewed against this backdrop. When employer controls are evaluated in the light of increased working hours, the demands of new technologies and the fact that in a majority of families with children both partners undertake paid work, it is easy to see why what I have called 'home space' has diminished.

We cannot retreat from technological changes, nor can we withdraw our nation from the global economy, yet the future and well-being of our lives is in our hands and we can take some steps to restore the balance between working life and home life. This can be achieved by strengthening home space. It is also my view that the law should be strengthened through the establishment of a legal right for professionals to be given work and training appropriate to their professional and related callings.

Strengthening home space

One way of strengthening home space is to increase the cultural and legal values which society places upon individual privacy. Moira Paterson of Monash University has argued for the enactment of strong privacy protection legislation which will cover not only the public sector but also the private sector. This issue has exercised the minds of various State and Federal Governments, but now is the time for some legislative action on a national level which will secure citizen privacy in the public and private sectors. On 1 February 1999 the New South Wales *Video Surveillance Act 1998*, which seeks to control covert video surveillance in workplaces, came into force and this is a useful measure which could be adopted by other parliaments.

Obviously comprehensive privacy legislation should protect purely private information which is in the hands of governments, corporations and agencies. I also believe that thought should be given to protecting from scrutiny and dissemination private email and other electronic communications. There are real technical difficulties here, but I contend that personal email should be as private as personal mail.

Another way of strengthening home space is to uphold the value of public holidays and of leave generally. Holidays like Australia Day and Anzac Day assist in building notions of community in our nation. There is much talk about flexibility and about weekends no longer being sacrosanct spaces upon which attendance at work may not intrude. Of course many hundreds of thousands of people go to work on Saturdays and we could not function as a global society without their weekend work. It is, however, timely to reaffirm the necessity for weekend family life and recreation. After all, weekends and evening hours are necessary to spend time with partners, children, other relatives and friends. It is at these times when community, sporting and school meetings take place and when community values and obligations are forged.

Finally, it is time for our governments and for the community to examine the plight of the growing number of professional, staff and other employees who are working for excessive hours. Traditionally, our labour laws have sought to protect standard employment by providing that where employees are required to work beyond their standard hours they must receive overtime pay. For professionals, however, our laws do not limit the hours which they may be required or feel impelled to work. An interesting contrast is seen in France where in May 1998, the French Parliament passed a measure to reduce the nation's working hours. It appears to apply to most employees and is due to come fully into operation in the year 2000. While this law may have been motivated, in part, to lessen unemployment through requiring employers to hire extra workers to take up the slack, it will be interesting to see how it will affect the working lives of professional employees in France.

The 1999 Working Time campaign of the Australian Council of Trade Unions is seeking to harness the concerns of ordinary

Australians about most aspects of working hours such as 12-hour shifts, broken shifts and minimum hours for part-time employees. More thought also needs to be given to discouraging excessive hours of work in order to protect our precious home space. I hope that my few words may encourage employees, employers and governments to discuss and to limit the harmful effects of the excessive working hours which are being undertaken by too many working Australians.

The right to be given appropriate work

In the previous chapter, I showed that many employees have little control over the nature and scope of the work they are required to perform. I believe the time is long overdue for the common law courts to hold that contracts for professional employees will contain an implied term to ensure that employees receive appropriate work and training to maintain and to enhance their skill levels and marketability as well as their dignity. The implication of such a term by force of law would go some way to redressing the gross imbalance between employee and employer obligations. Public sector professional employees are also in need of similar safeguards, but as this type of employment is governed by duties and obligations set out in statutes, legislation will be required to ensure that these professionals receive appropriate work.

Redrawing the boundaries

As previously mentioned, our judges do not operate in a vacuum because the rulings of our courts and industrial relations tribunals are in part shaped by our culture and by the collective values of our society. The enactment of comprehensive privacy legislation, together with greater social awareness of the importance of home space, will assist in the reshaping of employer and employee obligations to better balance working life and home life. When making rulings on the wording of written contracts, policies and/or codes of conduct, or when drawing implications about corporate image, our judges will do so against the backdrop of changed attitudes to privacy and to home space. This type of rethinking goes far beyond the bounds of employment law because personal privacy and adequate time to enjoy life are essential elements of a democratic Australia.

LIST OF CASES

Adami v Maison de Luxe Ltd (1924) 35 *Commonwealth Law Reports* p 143.

Anderson v Sullivan (1997) 78 *Federal Court Reports* p 380.

Applicant v Respondent, unreported, Australian Industrial Relations Commission, Deputy President Drake, Print P9973, 20 May 1998, on appeal to a Full Bench, Senior Deputy President MacBean, Deputy President Duncan, Commissioner Deegan, print R1221, 1 February 1999.

Associated Dominions Assurance Society v Andrew (1949) 49 *State Reports (New South Wales)* p 381.

Australian Manufacturing Workers' Union and Ors v Alcoa Australia Ltd and Ors (1996) 63 *Industrial Reports* p 138.

Australian Tramway Employees' Association v Brisbane Tramways Co Ltd (1912) 6 *Commonwealth Arbitration Reports* 35; on Judicial Review, *Australian Tramways Employees' Association v Prahran and Malvern Tramway Trust* (1913) 17 *Commonwealth Law Reports* p 680.

Blyth Chemicals Ltd v Bushnell (1933) 49 *Commonwealth Law Reports* p 66.

Boychuk v K J Symons Holdings Ltd [1977] *Industrial Relations Law Reports* p 395.

Collier v Sunday Referee Publishing Co Ltd [1940] 2 *King's Bench Reports* p 647.

Commissioner for Railways (NSW) v O'Donnell (1938) 60 *Commonwealth Law Reports* p 681.

Davis v Nokia Telecommunications Pty Ltd, unreported, Industrial Relations Court of Australia, Judicial Registrar Patch, 30 April 1996, on review *Nokia Telecommunications Pty Limited v Davis*, unreported, Industrial Relations Court of Australia, Wilcox CJ, 10 October 1996.

Family Leave Test Case (1994) 57 *Industrial Reports* p 121.

Federated Ship Painters and Dockers Union of Australia v Cockatoo Docks & Engineering Co Pty Ltd (1946) 57 *Commonwealth Arbitration Reports* p 137.

Gartside v Outram (1856) 26 *Law Journal Chancery Reports* p 113.

Hart v Jacobs and Ors (1981) 39 *Australian Law Reports* 209; on appeal *Australian Telecommunications Commission v Hart* (1982) 43 *Australian Law Reports* p 165.

Henry v Ryan [1963] *Tasmanian State Reports* p 90.

Hivac Ltd v Park Royal Scientific Instruments Ltd [1946] *Chancery Reports* 169.

Hozack v Church of Jesus Christ of Latter-Day Saints (1997) 79 *Federal Court Reports* p 441.

Hussein v Westpac Banking Corporation (1995) 59 *Idustrial Reports* p 103.

Initial Services Ltd v Putterill [1968] 1 *Queen's Bench Reports* p 296.

Jones v Lee [1980] *Industrial Cases Reports* p 310.

Lane v Fasciale and Anor (1993) 35 *Australian Industrial Law Review* paragraph 425.

Lion Laboratories Ltd v Evans [1984] 2 *All England Reports* p 417.

Malik and Mahmud v Bank of Credit and Commerce International [1998] *Appeal Cases* p 20.

Mann v The Capital Territory Health Commission (1981) 54 *Federal Law Reports* p 23.

McManus v Scott-Charlton (1996) 140 *Australian Law Reports* p 625.

Orr v The University of Tasmania (1957) 100 *Commonwealth Law Reports* p 526.

Pastry Cooks Employees, Biscuit Makers Employees and Flour and Sugar Goods Workers Union (NSW) v Gartrell White (No 3) (1990) 35 *Industrial Reports* p 70.

Part-Time Work Test Case (1998) 78 *Industrial Reports* p 172.

R v Teachers' Appeal Board; Ex parte Bilney (1983-1984) 6 *Industrial Reports* p 476.

Richards v BHP Iron Ore Ltd (1993) 73 *Western Australian Industrial Gazette* p 1863.

Rose v Telstra Corporation, unreported, Australian Industrial Relations Commission, Vice President Ross, Print Q9292, 4 December 1998.

Sim v Rotherham Metropolitan Borough Council [1986] 3 *Weekly Law Reports* p 851.

Transfield Pty Ltd re Dismissal of Union Delegate [1974] *Industrial Arbitration Reports of New South Wales* p 596

Turner v Mason (1845) 14 *Meeson and Welsby Reports* p 112 [153 *English Reports* p 411].

Wall v Westcott (1982) 1 *Industrial Reports* p 252.

Vabu Pty Ltd v Commissioner of Taxation (1996) 81 *Industrial Reports* p 150.

BIBLIOGRAPHY

Australian Centre for Industrial Relations Research and Training (University of Sydney) (1998) *Australia at Work: Just Managing?*, Prentice Hall, Sydney.

Blackstone, William (1978, a reprint of the 1783 9th ed) *Commentaries on the Laws of England*, Garland Publishers, New York.

Brooks, Adrian (1988) 'Myth and muddle — an examination of contracts for the performance of work', *University of New South Wales Law Journal*, vol 11, no 2, pp 48–101.

Collins, Hugh (1990) 'Independent contractors and the challenge of vertical disintegration of employment', *Oxford Journal of Legal Studies*, vol 10, pp 353–380.

Creighton, Breen; Ford, Bill and Mitchell, Richard (1993, 2nd ed) *Labour Law: Materials and Commentary*, The Law Book Co Ltd, Sydney.

Creighton, Breen and Stewart, Andrew (1994, 2nd ed) *Labour Law — An Introduction*, The Federation Press, Sydney.

Kahn-Freund, Otto (1977, 2nd ed) *Labour and the Law, the Hamlyn Lectures*, Stevens and Sons, London.

Kahn-Freund, Otto (1977) 'Blackstone's neglected child: the contract of employment', *Law Quarterly Review*, vol 93, pp 508–528.

Lewis, David (1996) 'Employment protection for whistleblowers: on what principles should Australian legislation be based?', *Australian Journal of Labour Law*, vol 9, pp 135–161.

Macken, James; O'Grady, Paul and Sappideen, Carolyn (1997, 4th ed) *Macken, McCarry and Sappideen's The Law of Employment*, The Law Book Co Ltd, Sydney.

MacNeil, Ian (1981) 'Economic analysis of contractual relations: its shortfalls and the need for a 'rich classificatory apparatus'', *Northwestern University Law Review*, vol 75, pp 1018–1063.

McCallum, Ron (1998) 'Employers' rights over workers outside the workplace', in *Legal Developments Affecting Human Resource Management in Australia: 6th Annual Labour Law Conference proceedings*, Australian Centre for Industrial

Relations Research and Training, University of Sydney, Working Paper No. 52, pp 1–6.

McCallum, Ron and McCarry, Greg (1995) 'Worker privacy in Australia', *Comparative Labour Law Journal*, vol 17, pp 13–37.

McCallum, Ron; McCarry, Greg and Ronfeldt, Paul (Eds) (1994) *Employment Security*, The Federation Press, Sydney.

McCallum, Ron and Pittard, Marilyn (1995, 3rd ed) *Australian Labour Law: Cases and Materials*, Butterworths, Sydney.

McCallum, Ron and Stewart, Andrew (1999) 'Employee loyalty in Australia', *Comparative Labour Law and Policy Journal*, (forthcoming).

McCarry, Greg (1981) 'The contract of employment and freedom of speech', *Sydney Law Review*, vol 9, pp 333–355.

McCarry, Greg (1998) 'Damages for breach of the employer's implied duty of trust and confidence', *Australian Business Law Review*, vol 26, pp 141–146.

Merritt, Adrian (1982) 'The historical role of law in the regulation of employment — abstentionist or interventionist', *Australian Journal of Law and Society*, vol 1, pp 56–86.

Mitchell, Richard (Ed) (1995) *Redefining Labour Law*, Centre for Employment and Labour Relations Law, University of Melbourne, Occasional Monograph series, Melbourne.

Moir, Matthew (1996) 'Individual and collective bargaining in Australian labour law: the CRA and Weipa cases', *Sydney Law Review*, vol 18, pp 350–371.

Naughton, Richard (1997) 'The implied obligation of mutual trust and confidence — a new cause of action for employees?', *Australian Journal of Labour Law*, vol 10, pp 287–291.

Paterson, Moira (1998) 'Privacy protection in Australia: the need for an effective private sector regime,' *Federal Law Review*, vol 26, pp 371–400.

Pocock, Barbara (1998) 'All change, still gendered: the Australian labour market in the 1990s', *Journal of Industrial Relations*, vol 40, pp 580–604.

Selznick, Philip (1969) *Law, Society and Industrial Justice*, Russell Sage Foundation, New York.

Stewart, Andrew (1988) 'Confidentiality and the employment relationship', *Australian Journal of Labour Law*, vol 1, pp 1–22.

Stewart, Andrew (1992) 'Ownership of property in the context of employment', *Australian Journal of Labour Law*, vol 5, pp 1–16.

Stewart, Andrew (1997) 'Drafting and enforcing post-employment restraints', *Australian Journal of Labour Law*, vol 10, pp 181–221.

Vandenheuvel, Audrey and Wooden, Mark (1995) 'Self-employed contractors in Australia: how many and who are they?', *Journal of Industrial Relations*, vol 37, pp 263–280.